BUYING CARS, TRUCKS, SUVS AND VANS

AMAZING SECRETS

TO

$AVE THOUSANDS

BY

LAWRENCE (LARRY) LEWIS

TABLE OF CONTENTS

FORWARD

I have been in new and used vehicle sales and management for over 35 years. I started in sales and after about six years, with a good understanding of the business, I became a used car manager. I then moved up to business manager, or as it's called at some dealerships, Finance Manager and the slang term in the business is F & I Manager (Finance and Insurance) and did that for about fifteen years.

I was responsible for vehicle lease and finance documentation, closing deals, sub-prime credit financing and selling insurances, (licensed by the state of Ohio). I also sold warranties and earned bank reserves for multi-franchise dealerships, representing Porsche, Audi, Mazda, Oldsmobile, Chevrolet, Buick, Ford, Lincoln Mercury, Chrysler, Plymouth, Dodge, Jeep, Nissan, Subaru and Volkswagon.

After that I worked for a man that owned three dealerships. I was the F & I Director, and responsible for training and development of all Business Managers (F & I Managers) at the three dealerships. Then on to F & I Consultant where I was an instructor and trainer responsible for training and assisting in the development of business managers in many, many automobile dealerships.

At almost sixty years old I moved to Florida and became an Internet Manager. Now I'm retired and still live in Florida.

I'm going to show you how to save a LOT of money. For example, not long ago, a customer came into a dealership to buy a new truck and trade in his old vehicle. By the time he left the dealership had made $10,000 profit on his purchase (can you believe that?!). I will show you how they did it and with my advice, **that will not happen to you**.

We are going to work your deal on paper before you ever go to the dealership. Just think of the money you will save in a lifetime of buying vehicles! I'm going to talk about the best time to buy, large rebates, how to save money when you finance a vehicle and much, much more!

This is a negotiation business and you're going to learn how. Think about this, they negotiate deals ten or twenty times a day or more; you do it only once ever three or four years! Using this book will put you on a level playing filed. I have spent many hours checking the internet and there is nothing out there that will compare to what you will learn from me and this book!

CHAPTER ONE

Finding A Vehicle You Like

With all the makes and models available, how do you narrow down your choice? To some extent, your lifestyle can help. Think about the activities you'll experience in the vehicle. If you have small children, you'll want to check safety features and find something roomy. You may want performance and style. If you have a job in sales and need room for clients or your vehicle has to haul or tow; the choices are pretty obvious.

With the large amount of vehicle information available on the internet and in books, many people still purchase vehicles after only a few days searching. This leaves a huge opportunity for a buyer to be sold a vehicle that they may not actually have wanted, rather than making an informed purchase decision.

Remember, as the buyer, you should be the one in control <u>throughout the entire process</u>. You should have already made your many choices along the way before you even step into a dealership. With so much reliable information available, even if you already have a strong preference about the vehicle you want, you should take some time to do research. Be open-minded - you may be pleasantly surprised by the outcome.

In helping family members and friends, I have found that the best way to find a <u>used vehicle</u> is on the internet, in the newspaper or by just driving and seeing a vehicle for sale.

Things to think about: buy out of season vehicles, such as a convertible in the winter. Buy late in the year when rebates or cash incentives are high. Always try to buy the last day or two of the month or at the end of the year.

Don't forget about insurance - you should check on your new premium or rate once you have chosen a vehicle to make sure it's not going to be much higher than your old one.

For example; I remember a time when I sold a young man a performance car. He traded in a little 4-cylinder truck. We completed the deal and he called his insurance company to bind coverage - not even asking how much! A week and a half later he received his bill in the mail that was three times higher than his 4-cylinder truck!

Don't forget about quality - an online analysis of how your favorite vehicles rates in quality can be a true eye-opener.

The opinion of experts is another tool you should use on the internet. It's another way to gain confidence in the vehicle you're going to purchase so spend some time reading what the experts have to say.

Let's pause a moment and get our ducks in a row for later when you purchase. In all my years working in financing, 98% of the time credit unions had the lowest interest rates.

Now once in a while the manufacturer will have special rates and that's great, but if not, you'll be going to a bank or the dealer will arrange financing for you. I believe credit unions over all have the lowest rates, so you need to join one now, when you're ready to purchase you're already a member of a credit union.

While I'm giving my opinions, let's talk about gas mileage. Owning my first car to the vehicle I have today, having bought gas for them all, the price has always gone up. Don't buy a vehicle with a larger engine than you need - gas prices will continue to rise!

Alright, you have picked three or four vehicles you like. Let's go on the test drive. Example: I'll never forget the time I sold a man a vehicle that he drove around the block and then bought. About six months later he came back in and said the seat hurt his back after he drove more than thirty miles. He lost thousands of dollars to trade again so quickly. The test drive is very important. Tell them you need to go show your spouse or you want to make sure it fits okay in your garage, just drive it awhile to be sure. If you can, drive it overnight - some dealers will do this.

Also, on the test drive, take time to sit in <u>all</u> the seats, front and back. Have someone else drive and see what it's like to ride in the vehicle.

Stop somewhere and walk around the vehicle. Look it over, do the exterior and interior colors match? Be sure and drive the vehicle on city streets and highways. Don't rush the process!

Check the comfort of the ride, vibrations, handling and look for blind spots when backing up. Be sure to note how the vehicle responds when you push the accelerator pedal and how the brakes feel when you press the brake pedal.

Now if this is a used vehicle you're test driving and it's the one you want to buy you **must** take it to a mechanic to be looked at. It's a small price to pay for peace of mind. How are the tires and how's the paint work?

A vehicle purchase is a large investment. Make sure you spend enough time really looking it over. Then consider one last thing: your intuition. If you are uneasy about the vehicle, follow your instincts. A vehicle purchase decision is too important (and too expensive) to undertake without total confidence.

Find a very good research web site - one that will let you compare 4 vehicles at one time. They should show pricing, dealer costs, compare features, technical specifications, safety and reviews, ratings, customer incentives like rebates, special finance rates - some as low as zero A.P.R., military incentives and college student cash back.

Now let's cover depreciation of your new vehicle. Some vehicles hold their value very well, while others depreciate very quickly. When you trade this vehicle you will want a great trade-in value, one that's not going to drop so quickly.

Example: a person buys a $40,000 SUV. In four years they decide to trade it in. When they visit the dealer they find out that their four year old SUV is only worth $10,000. The obvious result is $40,000 - $10,000 = $30,000. The SUV cost them a loss value of **$30,000**.

To have a rough idea of what the vehicle you are planning to buy will be worth in four years from now, look up the current trade-in value of a four year old vehicle of the same model. You can find all the info you need on the internet then compare which new vehicle holds its value best.

Another idea: if you need to rent a car for any reason, rent the model that you are considering to buy. This will give you a lot better idea how it will drive, handle and if it's too large or small, etc.

Now a few things you must make note of if you're buying a used vehicle. You <u>must</u> run a 'Car Fax'. In most cases you'll find a lot of the history of the vehicle. Look it over good, but remember, bad items may not be on the Car Fax if the work or problem was done in a small garage or shop.

<u>Don't</u> work numbers while you're looking and test driving. You're not ready for that yet.

Contact the internet manager at all dealerships for test drives and information. That's where we are going to get our best deal later and with less hassle. Also remember for most of your research use the internet.

My goal is to help you save thousands of dollars. <u>Please</u> follow my advice. Now do your homework and to help, use the following short recap.

IMPORTANT ITEMS TO REMEMBER

❖ Check Safety Features (Internet)

❖ Do Your Research (Internet)

❖ Check Quality (Internet & Test Drive)

❖ Get The Opinion Of Experts (Internet)

❖ You Want A Good Gas Mileage Engine

❖ Look For Special Rebates, Incentives, Interest Rates, From The Factory

❖ Do All Test Drives and Dealership Research With The Internet Manager

❖ Make Sure The Vehicle Is Comfortable And Look It Over Carefully

❖ Buy Out Of Season, End Of Month Or End Of Year

❖ Check Depreciation Of The New Vehicle Over 4 Years (Internet)

❖ Think About Renting Your Favorite Vehicle

❖ Have The Used Car Inspected By A Mechanic

❖ You Must Run A Car Fax

❖ Check The Cost Of Your New Insurance

- ❖ Check Interest Rates At The Credit Union (Become A Member)

- ❖ Remember - Don't Work Numbers Yet

- ❖ **YOU ARE IN CONTROL!**

YOUR NOTES

_____

_____

_____

_____

_____

_____

_____

_____

_____

_____

_____

_____

_____

_____

_____

_____

_____

_____

CHAPTER TWO

Cost Of Your New Vehicle

A new vehicle is second only to a home as the most expensive purchase many consumers make according to the National Automobile Dealers Association and the average price of a new vehicle sold in the United States is about $28,000. That's why it's important to know how to make a good deal!

As I have said before, if you buy a new vehicle about every four years for the rest of your life and use my book, think of the thousands of dollars you will have saved! My goal in this chapter is to help you find out what is the lowest price you can buy your new vehicle for.

Okay, you have found a new vehicle or vehicles that you like. Let's go to the internet to find dealer invoice cost. There are quite a few sites to choose from, so choose your favorite. My personal favorite is kellybluebook.com because you can put as many as four vehicles in at one time and compare invoice and MSRP (retail price).

You can also see the incentive and rebates on each vehicle. While you're checking out the site, please note that the site should also tell you the country of origin and factory warranty on each vehicle.

Now that we know the dealer invoice cost and all the rebates and incentives that are available, subtract all those rebates and incentives from the dealer invoice. We are going to use this as our 'buying figure'. Write this figure down and save it. This buying figure will be used later during your negotiations.

A reminder for you - there are vehicle buying services on the internet. **<u>DON'T USE THEM!</u>** The fee they get from the dealer could affect your best buying figure. For research, only use the ones that are free and don't ask for your name, address or credit card number.

Some helpful information that you need to know and that we are going to discuss is the money that dealers make that you <u>DON'T</u> know about.

I feel the most important one is called '***holdback***'. This is a 2% to 3% of the vehicle MSRP or invoice, paid to the dealer by the factory quarterly each year.

At one time, who knows when, I suspect the dealers contacted the factory and said to the effect of, "I'm getting killed out here, everyone knows my invoice cost! You've got to find ways to put money in my pocket that consumers can't find out about! If you don't help, you're not going to have stores to sell your product."

Years ago there was a much greater gap between the retail price (MSRP) and the dealer invoice. That gap has been shortened to give the dealers and factories more room for hidden incentives to the dealer. Let's talk about some of these incentives to the dealer.

Usually, the dealer incentives of today are not tied to the sale of any one specific vehicle. Instead, they are geared to overall dealership objectives set by the factory on a dealership by dealership basis.

Dealers can earn significant cash bonuses by reaching these unknown sales targets. There is no way to learn where any dealership stands on the earning of these cash incentives.

But you and I know they get extra money from the factory!

The solution to this problem can put money in your pocket. Contact three or four different Internet Managers at different dealerships for numbers, which almost always smokes out some of these incentives by making dealers bid competitively for your business. Some dealers may even lose money on your deal in an effort to reach sales targets that will earn them big bonus checks from the factory!

Now let's finish this plan by talking about the Dealership Internet Sales Department. A Dealership Internet Sales Department prices it's vehicles to maximize the number of vehicles it sells. The more they sell, the more the factory allocation increases.

To level the playing field for your negotiation, come into the dealership through the internet department. It tells the dealer that you have done your research and you know about rebates, holdback and their other incentives.

Later in Chapter Six: <u>Understanding The Numbers - Working The Deal On Paper</u>, you are going to take your buying figure (dealer invoice minus rebates and incentives) and contact three or four dealer internet departments, buying your vehicle for the lowest bid, below the buying figure!

Remember, hard to get vehicles or very good selling, popular vehicles will be much more difficult to buy for lower prices.

If you read and understand this entire book and follow my advice <u>before</u> you start any of your negotiating, then my story about the customer that let the dealership make $10,000 profit on them (in the forward of this book) - **won't happen to you!**

IMPORTANT ITEMS TO REMEMBER

- ❖ A New Vehicle Is The Second Most Expensive Item You Buy

- ❖ Get The Absolute Lowest Price You Can

- ❖ Don't Use An Internet Buying Service

- ❖ The Dealer Earns Extra Money From The Factory

- ❖ You Must Negotiate All You Can

- ❖ Use The Dealership Internet Department

- ❖ Popular Vehicles Will Be Harder To Get A Good Deal On

CHAPTER THREE

What You Should Pay For A Used Vehicle

My goal in this chapter is to show you a range in numbers of about what you should pay for a used vehicle. You should have no problems if you follow my advice. What you are about to learn could save you thousands of dollars.

As I have said before, please read this entire book before you venture out to buy your vehicle.

Understanding all the various factors that have an effect on used vehicle prices can be a challenging process. Trying to accurately judge the resale value of a specific vehicle based on mileage, condition and features and to have a solid grasp of used vehicle pricing issues can help you make informed and intelligent decisions as you search for that perfect used vehicle.

An important part of the used vehicle buying process is determining and settling on a fair and reasonable price that can mean the difference between being satisfied with your purchase or feeling like you may have been taken advantage of. Most people don't have the experience or knowledge of the used vehicle market to make the right decisions, but as you read this chapter, you will have a very good idea of <u>what to pay for a used vehicle</u>.

Using the process you are about to learn could, over your lifetime, save you enough money to actually pay for a vehicle!

Let's talk about what can lower the value of a vehicle. Probably the most significant reason would be high miles, but don't worry, the web sites we are going to use will factor this in for us.

They won't factor in a wreck or if it has a salvage title. In this day of using **CAR FAX** to check vehicles on the internet you will find this out, and of course, lower what you are willing to pay.

We should talk about a wrecked vehicle first; minor damage won't affect the way a vehicle runs and drives. A salvage title on a newer vehicle, I think, can be a bad idea and a risk. But on a nice older vehicle that's only worth $5,000 or $6,000 it can be a good deal.

With that in mind, think about this, if that vehicle was in a wreck and the damage was $4,700 (which would not take much damage at body shop rates) the insurance company would total it because that's all it's worth.

Now let's say the damage was not serious, just a trunk lid and fender or hood and bumper or fender and grill, that vehicle is still okay as long as you make sure all paint and body parts look good.

Any used vehicle you're thinking of buying should be checked by a good mechanic and any vehicle that has been wrecked, should be checked by a body repair shop.

The salvage vehicle we just talked about may be worth $6,000 normally and you should be able to buy it for $4,000 - a very good savings. Especially if it has low miles.

In fact, any vehicle in my opinion that you buy, should have low miles, so you can get a lot of use out of it. And to really get your money's worth on any vehicle, you should drive it till the doors fall off (an old saying). Buying vehicles every couple of years is a money losing proposition.

Alright, let's assume you have found a vehicle you like by looking on the internet at used cars, in the newspaper, or you drove by one that caught your eye. If it's at a dealership I strongly suggest you work with the internet manager - you'll have less hassle.

Now go look at and drive the vehicle. You need to know the condition it's in to figure value. Also check the mileage and good or bad tires. If it runs good mechanically, be sure to have a mechanic check it over. Please make note of all equipment and options the vehicle has. We will need that information next.

The used vehicle book out process is a quick and simple one. Using it, we will have our approximate value. Used vehicle values can be found within minutes when you use **Edmunds** and **NADA** web sites on your computer.

Let's start with NADA - pull them up on your computer.

1. Select MAKE, then click

2. Select YEAR, then click

3. Select MODEL, then click

NOTE: if your vehicle has special model markings like LS, GS, SS, Sport, etc... be sure and mark the right one as this will affect the value.

4. Select 2-Door or 4-Door

5. Now enter the mileage

6. Scroll down and select any optional equipment

7. Next hit CONTINUE

8. It now says PRICING with four columns

   A.   Rough Trade-In Value

   B.   Average Trade-In Value

   C.   Clean Value Trade In

   D.   Clean Value Retail

Look at the bottom of each column for the total price - that's our value with optional equipment, miles, etc.

As you look at the column marked average trade in and clean trade in, that's about what the dealer has in the vehicle as far as money.

Now average out the two numbers and write down that figure. You will also see retail value - that's about what the dealer will be asking for the vehicle, but we want it for much less that that!

Okay, let's go over to the EDMUNDS site and do the same thing.

First pick USED CARS - scroll down and select APPRAISE in the Appraise and Research Section

Then select MAKE - when the new screen comes up, select your YEAR

Select MODEL

NOTE: if your vehicle has special model markings like LS, GS, SS, Sport, etc... be sure and mark the right one as this will affect the value.

Select 2-Door or 4-Door

Now scroll down and select BUY

Next enter the mileage

Scroll down and select any optional equipment

Next hit CONDITION

Now select PRICING REPORT

Scroll down and you will see your Pricing Report Totals

>   A.   Trade-In

>   B.   Private Party

>   C.   Dealer Retail

Look at the bottom of each column for the total price. Trade-In is what your vehicle is worth wholesale and is about what a dealer will have invested in that vehicle - write this figure down.

Now look back at the figure you wrote down from NADA. This figure, together with the figure from EDMUNDS, is about what the dealer has invested in the vehicle.

Set your figures aside for now - we will use them in Chapter Six, <u>Understanding The Numbers And Working The Deal On Paper Yourself</u>.

But remember, wholesale is the low figure and retail is the high figure. You want to try and buy for wholesale (low) and trade for or sell your trade for retail (high).

IMPORTANT ITEMS TO REMEMBER

- ❖ Choose A Vehicle In Good Shape

- ❖ Buy A Vehicle With Low Mileage

- ❖ Have The Vehicle Checked By A Mechanic

- ❖ Have The Vehicle Checked By A Body Repair Shop

- ❖ Ask For A **CAR FAX**

- ❖ Use NADA and/or EDMUNDS web sites to help you determine the value of the vehicle

YOUR NOTES

CHAPTER FOUR

Your Trade-In Value

If you're considering trading in your old vehicle in order to reduce the price of your new purchase, it is important to find out the accurate <u>used vehicle trade-in value</u>. Besides helping you decide whether or not you actually want to trade it in or sell it yourself, an accurate trade-in value will also insure that you get a fair price from the dealer when it comes time to trade it in.

One of the first things you should do is analyze your vehicle. Does it run and operate smoothly? Do you need tires? How does the paint look on the vehicle? How clean is it overall? The better all these items are, the more you'll get from the dealer. And if you choose to sell it yourself, it will sell quicker and for more money!

When you are considering trading in your used vehicle, you should know the difference between the <u>trade-in value</u> and the <u>retail value</u>.

The trade-in value is what a dealer will give you for your vehicle on a trade for another vehicle minus clean up costs, mechanic repairs, tire replacement and paint work. Also note that most dealers will try to give you a little less, just to have more money to work with when they sell your trade-in.

Remember, when you're negotiating, the dealer will start very low on your trade-in value and only come up when you force him, but he will come up!

The retail value is what a dealer could expect to sell your trade-in vehicle for. Most dealers almost always add $1,000 or more over retail price. Just to have more money to work with.

Now let's go back to the computer and do the same process as we did for Chapter Three: What You Should Pay For A Used Vehicle. Put your trade-in as the vehicle for appraisal.

NOTE: Remember when you select the condition of your vehicle be realistic. Most vehicles are in the Good or Poor column. To be in the Excellent column they must be in like new condition.

Let's start with NADA - pull them up on your computer.

1. Select MAKE, then click

2. Select YEAR, then click

3. Select MODEL, then click

NOTE: if your vehicle has special model markings like LS, GS, SS, Sport, etc... be sure and mark the right one as this will affect the value.

4. Select 2-Door or 4-Door

5. Now enter the mileage

6. Scroll down and select any optional equipment

7. Next hit CONTINUE

8. It now says PRICING with four columns

   A. Rough Trade-In Value

   B. Average Trade-In Value

   C. Clean Value Trade In

   D. Clean Value Retail

On the left side you will see a column for three choices - Rough Trade-In, Average Trade-In and Clean Trade-In.

Rough trade-in value applies if your vehicle is in bad or 'rough' shape. Average trade-in is if your vehicle is in useable condition, but needs cosmetic repairs. Clean trade-in is for when your vehicle looks almost new.

Choose whichever condition your vehicle is in - and be honest with yourself! Write down whichever figure your vehicle is in and save it.

On the right you will find the Clean Retail figure. Write this figure down and save it as well.

Now let's go to the EDMUNDS site on the computer and put your trade-in on their web site for appraisal. We hope to get close to retail for your trade-in depending on condition.

First pick USED CARS.

Scroll down and select APPRAISE in the Appraise and Research Section

Then select MAKE - select YEAR

Select MODEL

NOTE: if your vehicle has special model markings like LS, GS, SS, Sport, etc... be sure and mark the right one as this will affect the value.

Select 2-Door or 4-Door

Now scroll down and select BUY

Next enter the mileage

Scroll down and select any optional equipment

Next hit CONDITION

Scroll down and you will see your Pricing Report Totals

A.   Trade-In

B.   Private Party

C.   Dealer Retail

Look to the right and write down the Dealer Retail value price. This is what you should try to get from the dealer for your trade.

Take your retail numbers from the NADA site and average them out. Take your retail numbers from the EDMUNDS site and average them out. This is about the amount you will get for your trade-in if you sell it. Always start higher so you can come down if you need to.

Now looking at the trade-in figure from both sites, NADA and EDMUNDS, you'll see your average trade-in number. Working with a dealership, they will try to deduct about $500 on low priced vehicles for trade-in and $1,500 or so on higher priced vehicles. The reason for this is so they have more to work with when they 'Retail' your vehicle. They will also deduct for tires, paint work, mechanic repairs and clean up.

As you can see by all of this, you will almost assuredly get more for your trade-in vehicle if you sell it yourself.

The web sites of NADA and EDMUNDS are the sites I prefer, but you are certainly free to choose any sites you personally like. You will come up with about the same numbers with whichever sites you use.

Now that you know the approximant vehicle trade-in value and retail value, you can determine if you want to trade at a dealer or sell it yourself.

Keep in mind, dealers may compete a little over the trade-in value of your vehicle. The more dealers you visit the more you will learn about the value of your used vehicle.

IMPORTANT ITEMS TO REMEMBER

❖ Analyze Your Trade-In Vehicles' Condition - Be Honest And Realistic About The Condition Of Your Vehicle

❖ Get An Accurate Used Vehicle Trade-In Value

❖ Get An Accurate Retail Vehicle Value

❖ Consider Selling The Vehicle Yourself - You'll Probably Get More Money

YOUR NOTES

_____

_____

_____

_____

_____

_____

_____

_____

_____

_____

_____

_____

_____

_____

_____

_____

_____

_____

CHAPTER FIVE

Let's Go Over Leasing

To lease, or not to lease, that is the question! I hope to give you the answer in this chapter.

Please read it slowly and think about each sentence, paragraph and page. Let it soak into your mind. There is a lot of information contained in here for your mind to soak in!

Leasing is the most complex part to know and understand when getting your vehicle. All the terms and meanings of words are very different than with a purchase.

Many vehicle consumers don't know or understand how vehicle leasing really works, therefore, don't know how to determine if it's right for them.

Many people now leasing are overpaying because they didn't know how to get a good deal or how to recognize a bad one. Others who could greatly benefit from leasing are shying away because they don't understand it or have misconceptions about it.

When you agree to lease a vehicle, the dealer must attempt to assign the lease with the factory, the bank or sometimes a lease company. In most cases it will be with the factory or manufacturer because the residual (lease end value) will be the highest. The higher the residual the less you pay.

In Chapter 1: Finding A Vehicle You Like, I recommended using a credit union for financing, but unfortunately, in most cases, they don't do leases. Check credit unions in your area to see if they will.

Why lease? The term is shorter in most cases, only 24 to 48 months, which is how long some people will keep a vehicle. This way you only pay for the portion of the vehicle that you are using. The value of the vehicle remaining at the end of the lease you never pay for.

You are paying for the depreciation only, not the full price of the vehicle. Because of this, in most cases, you will need very good credit in order to qualify for a lease.

Before we delve too deep into the world of leasing I want to give you the meanings of the important words and phrases used in most leases.

Residual Value

The percentage of the MSRP (window sticker) that the Leasing Company figures to be the value of the vehicle at the end of the lease.

Residualized Accessories

Items added to your vehicle that raises the value and the residual value such as sunroof, spoiler, stereo upgrades, etc. These may lower your payment.

Gross Capitalized Cost

This is the purchase price of the vehicle.

Capitalized Cost Reduction

This refers to rebates, trade-in and cash paid down.

Net Capitalized Cost

This is your new total price after all rebates, trade-in and cash paid down.

Money Factor

This is the interest or finance charge on your lease.

Leasee

This is you!

Leasor

The leasing company

MSRP

This is the window sticker price

Acquisition Fee

This is a fee to do your lease. In most cases, it's extra charges or profit to the dealer or leasor. If you shop around it may be reduced or eliminated. If you don't watch out, some dealers may mark up more profit here.

Security Deposit

This is usually equivalent to the monthly payment, rounded up to the next $25. For example, your payment is $335 a month, security deposit is $350. This may be waived for some previous lease customers.

Disposition Fee

This is a lease company fee for transporting the vehicle to the auction at the end of the lease. Some lease companies do not charge this fee. If you buy the vehicle at the end of the lease there is no disposition fee.

Excess Mileage Fee

This fee is paid at the end of the lease for mileage in excess of the specified miles allowed.

Early Termination Fee

This is a fee for breaking the lease early. Read the lease contract carefully, looking for this, before signing.

Closed End Lease

You will want this lease. This is a lease where the actual value of the vehicle at the end of the lease is at the risk of the lease company - not the customer.

Open End Lease

You do not want this lease. This lease is where the value of the vehicle at the end of the lease is the responsibility of the customer.

Pre-Paid Lease

For people who have below average credit, but have the cash needed, this is great. You pay all your payments up front. This is very good for people that pay cash in full for their vehicle. If you paid cash for a pre-paid lease, your cost would be much less than a full retail purchase. It's a very good deal.

Normal Wear And Tear

Your vehicle should be in average condition when you return it, showing only normal wear and tear. For example, if your lease was for three years, whatever would normally wear (such as tires, worn seats, faded paint) is okay. Anything else that is broken, dented, seat tears, or windshield cracked or chipped will be your responsibility.

Most people object to leasing because of false assumptions or bad experiences. Some of these problems could have been avoided if the customer had been more aware of what a lease is all about.

With the average lease you are limited to what you can change or add on the vehicle. You can't paint flames on the sides, add on hood scoops or superchargers.

Some leases limit where you can travel to (long distances) in the vehicle. Be more cautious with your lease. Check all fine print on the front and back of the lease. Ask questions if you feel uneasy about something or need to clarify a point.

Leased vehicles generally require more insurance coverage. This is because the lease company is actually the owner of the vehicle. The lease company can be held liable for your negligence.

You may also pay less in sales tax. Every state is different, but generally, you only pay tax on the portion of the vehicle you are using, not the total value.

One of the drawbacks of leasing is it's very hard to get out of one once you have made the commitment. Talk to your leasor (leasing company) to make sure your comfortable with their program.

Think about this for a moment - on a lease, the more it's worth at the end, the less you pay. With that fact in mind, try to pick a vehicle that is known to hold its value. Foreign vehicles tend to lease better than domestic vehicles due to the strong residual values. Foreign vehicles generally hold their value better, but not always.

With that thought in mind, a vehicle with a sunroof, leather interior, four-wheel drive, etc. is worth more and its residual value will be higher - so you'll pay less.

A great benefit to leasing is the tax advantage. When you lease and write off the vehicle as a business expense, you can generally write off the entire payment. The reason is that on a lease you are paying for the depreciation, which should be tax deductible.

On the average lease your miles per year are between 12,000 and 15,000. If you think you are going to drive more than that, buy extra miles at the beginning of your lease. They cost less at the beginning than they do at the end. If you go over your miles and if your vehicle value is high, you may be able to trade it in and not have to pay a mileage fee. You should have that option.

Let's talk about money factor, which is your interest charge or finance charge. It should be a number like .00271. This can only be converted to a percentage rate by taking that number and multiplying it by 2400 (.00271 x 2400 = 6.5%). Be careful here - the dealer can earn extra money sometimes by raising the money factor.

A few items to make note of:

With a lease there is no being upside down on your vehicle, as could happen with a purchase.

A lease is very good because in most cases, you should have very little maintenance. Regular maintenance should be covered by the factory warranty!

Don't forget at the end of your lease to get your security deposit back.

Most leasors want your first monthly payment the day you sign your lease agreement.

Some new vehicle dealers will lease one or two year old, low mileage used vehicle. When I was in the business it wasn't done much because most people didn't know it could be done! This doesn't imply that the new vehicle dealer <u>has</u> to lease you a used, low mileage vehicle, simply that it is done on occasion. It doesn't hurt to ask!

When you lease a vehicle you should negotiate the purchase price (gross capitalized) cost just like you would on a regular purchase.

I'm going to close this chapter with a true story. Read on, and if you now have an understanding of leasing, you won't believe this. In most cases, it's not a good deal to buy your lease at the end, but my story is an example of when it is a good deal.

A few years back, a customer came in and we worked a lease agreement on a vehicle that had a MSRP (window sticker) of about $60,000. Now this customer either owned or co-owned a company of his own. While working the lease on my computer, he asked if I could change the residual factor (lease end value) and make it lower. I called the factory and they said yes, but you can't raise the residual value, which I already knew.

Normally this vehicle would be worth about $35,000 at the lease end. We lowered the residual factor to make it worth about $10,000 at lease end.

Now this raised the payment quite a bit, but he didn't care since his company was making the payment. At the end of the lease, he bought the vehicle for $10,000 (worth $35,000) for his son.

His company paid for that large depreciation, but got a tax write-off for it. WOW !!!

IMPORTANT ITEMS TO REMEMBER

❖ Know And Fully Understand The Principles Of Leasing

❖ Know And Understand The Meaning Of The Commonly Used Phrases And Words

❖ Check Your Credit Union To See If They Will Finance A Lease

❖ Leasing Is Very Good If You Only Keep Your Vehicles A Short Time

❖ Your Vehicle Insurance May Go Up

❖ In Most Cases The Tax Savings Are Very Good

❖ Make Sure You Buy Extra Miles Up Front If You Think You'll Need Them

YOUR NOTES

CHAPTER SIX

Understanding The Numbers - Working The Deal On Paper

My goal in this chapter is to help you put all the numbers together for your vehicle purchase. Later when you are at the dealership it can get confusing very fast with the wheeling and dealing. Remember, keep the pace slower, so you know and understand exactly what's happening. When you're making your deal, if it's going too fast or you don't feel comfortable, leave the dealership. Come back another day. The more you do this, the more you learn and the better the deal!

Most dealerships work your deal with what is called a 4-Square. The ones not using the 4-Square will probably use a Buyers Order or just a piece of paper. Whatever they use, there are four major items shown. I'm going to show you the 4-Square and those four items.

#1 Vehicle Purchase Price	#2 Trade-In
#3 Down Payment	#4 Monthly Payments

Now I want you to draw your own 4-Square on a piece of paper.

1   Vehicle Purchase Price

Look at your notes - if you're buying a new vehicle, the number we want to use here is from Chapter Two, your <u>Buying Figure</u>. That is the dealer invoice minus all rebates and incentives. If you're buying a used vehicle, the number we want to use here is from Chapter Three, the average trade-in or wholesale trade-in. Write in square # 1 (in your 4-Square) the number that you are using.

2   Trade-In

If you are not trading in a vehicle but selling the trade-in yourself, just skip # 2 and leave it blank. If you are trading, the number we want to use here is from Chapter Four, the average price we figured from NADA and EDMUNDS. This was the average figure between wholesale and retail or trade-in and retail - write it in square # 2.

<u>Note:</u> while we are discussing trade-ins, remember, that if you have a payoff due on your old loan you will only receive the amount left after your original loan has been satisfied. For instance, let's say you owe $4,000 on your original loan and the dealer offers you $10,000 trade-in. That will leave only $6,000 to be applied against your new loan.

3 - Down Payment

They are always going to try to get you to put a down payment on your vehicle. If you do, your monthly payments will be less and they know that will make you happy! If you don't want to give a down payment, I'll show you shortly what your payment will be without any money down.

Note: remember back in Chapter One: Finding A Vehicle You Like, I told you to get your loan at your credit union or bank. If you have not already done it, stop and do it now! It's the cheapest way for you. You'll see why in Chapter Seven: Let's Learn About Front End And Back End Profit.

4   Monthly Payment

The last of the 4 Square is monthly payment. They will always try to keep you away from # 1, the purchase price and # 2, trade-in because most people just care about payment. If they do that successfully, you may pay more for the vehicle or take less for your trade-in because the payment is within your budget.

But with their seventy-two (72) month or eighty-four (84) month financing, you're paying a TON of interest to the financing institution. We don't want that, do we? That's why we want to arrange our own financing with our credit union or bank.

While we are talking about monthly payment amounts, I'm going to show you how to get an idea of how to figure that.

On the average, a $10,000 loan financed for sixty (60) months would be about $200 a month, give or take a little. With that in mind, a $30,000 loan for sixty (60) months would be about $600 a month, give or take a little bit.

You don't want to let the dealers try to work with you on # 3 - Down Payment or # 4 - Monthly Payment. You should have all that taken care of with your credit union or bank.

You just want to get your best purchase price and your best trade-in price that you can.

As the dealers negotiate, they will start as high as they can with the purchase price (Square # 1) - and be careful here - they may have used an add-on window sticker.

They add on the cost of pin stripes, rust-proofing, fabric sealant, undercoating and a long list of other items. Simply tell them which of these that you want, if any, and which you don't. Go back to your MSRP (window sticker price). The items we just covered are great profit items for the dealer.

As the dealer negotiates your trade-in (Square # 2), they will always start very low and go up VERY slowly. As you will see, starting very high on the purchase price allows them to come down very slowly. That's their game, come down slowly (on purchase price) and go up slowly (on your trade-in amount).

Your game is exactly the opposite of theirs. You want to start low on your purchase price (square # 1) and start high on your trade-in (square # 2) amount.

In closing this chapter, when a deal is worked on a 4 Square, it shows no sales tax, license and plate transfer fees or title transfer fees.

They will surprise you with a "dealer fee", anywhere from $100 to $500. This is almost always total profit for them. Be careful, this "dealer fee" should not be more than $30 to $50 to notarize and transfer your title and memo title, etc.

Note: your best negotiated price (# 1 Purchase Price) can be used as your Gross Capitalized Cost (Purchase Price) on a lease.

IMPORTANT ITEMS TO REMEMBER

❖ Understand The Numbers.

❖ Work The Deal On Paper Yourself.

❖ Keep The Pace As **SLOW** As You Need It To Be When You're Working Your Deal.

❖ Make Your Own 4-Square, Know And Understand It.

❖ If You Have A Payoff Due On Your Trade-In, It <u>MUST</u> Be Paid.

❖ Don't Put Anymore Money Down Than You Want To.

❖ Find Out From Your Credit Union Or Bank What The Monthly Payment Is On The Amount You're Financing.

❖ Find Out From Your Financial Institution What Their Finance Charge Will Be Over The Life Of The Loan.

YOUR NOTES

CHAPTER SEVEN

Let's Learn About Front End
And Back End Profit

My goal in this chapter is to make you aware of another profit center dealers have that most buyers are not knowledgeable of. After reading this chapter you will understand why I want you to arrange your own financing with your credit union or bank. I strongly encourage you to pay close attention and follow my advice.

The term Front End Profit means profit that's made when they sell you any vehicle, new or used. Example: you buy a vehicle and the profit is $1,500, then you buy a cap or add a bed liner for your truck, or perhaps you upgrade the radio, change tires and wheels or add a hood scoop, etc. on your car, van or SUV. All the profit made when your salesman sells you the vehicle and everything that he sells you added on or changed at the time of sale is Front End Profit. That could now be $2,500 after some of these adds.

Let's call Front End Profit phase one. Most people think they're done now and kind of let down their guard. Well, not so, the next place you're going to be taken to is the Business Office to finish your title work, take care of financing or pay cash and receipt the money.

Now we are going to phase two. This is where the Back End Profit is made. And in most cases, the profit here can be more than they made selling you the vehicle. Example: you're financing your vehicle and you let the Finance and Insurance Manager (F & I Manager) in the Business Office arrange your loan for you.

In most cases, he will earn money from the lender for sending in your loan to them. That could be anywhere from 2% to sometimes 6% of the amount financed.

If you financed $25,000, that would be $500 profit at 2%. Now let's say the F & I Manager earned 6% on your loan that would be $1,500 at 6% he earned for sending in your loan, not bad - hah!

If you arrange your loan with a credit union or your bank you could save money on the interest rate, so the dealer won't earn the 2% or more.

Now let's say that they talk you into buying paint sealant, or rust-proofing and undercoating. And that would give them a few hundred dollars more back end profit.

Or maybe you bought GAP Coverage, that if your vehicle is wrecked it pays the difference between what the insurance company gives you and what you owe the bank for your loan pay-off. (You can buy this for much less from your credit union.) They have more back end profit.

What if they talk you into buying Credit Life, Accident, Health and Disability coverage - Hundreds more back end profit! Or they talk you into a fancy alarm or glass etching for theft protection. Hundreds more <u>back end profit</u>! And the list goes on and on.

I think there's something you need to know at this point. All states are different about controlling prices on the items you can buy in the Business Office. But most of these items, if you want them are negotiable.

The first one is extended warranty coverage; second item is GAP coverage, third would be paint sealant, fourth is rust-roofing undercoating and fifth would be alarms systems and glass etching theft protection.

While we are on this subject of negotiating, as I think you already know, those items you bought on the <u>front end profit</u> mostly can also be up for negotiation.

Also, as with almost all these items, if you don't like their price, you can shop around at other dealers for a better price. (The dealer you're at will hate this - be sure to tell them!)

Now a quick point about extended warranty protection - I, myself, would never buy anything but <u>manufacturer issued warranties</u>. They're recognized by every dealer in the country of that make.

Now we have talked about <u>front end profit</u> and <u>back end profit</u>, let's cover over all dealership profit. I want you to think about the whole dealership as four businesses in one.

First, of course, we have the Sales Department, then we have the Service Department, then the Parts Department and also the Paint and Body Shop.

As you can see, it's very important for the Sales Department to keep selling vehicles so the other departments are kept busy and profitable. So think about this as you're working your deal later - they really, really need your business!

The Business Manager is one of the most important people in the dealership. He can make profit appear faster (one hour or so) and he actually makes more profit from his products than most salesman make on the sale of the vehicle in most dealerships.

With dealers being more and more competitive in these lean times, profit is sometimes sacrificed in the <u>front end</u> of the vehicle with the intent to make it up in the <u>back end</u> by the <u>Business Manager</u>.

With this in mind, <u>never</u> tell them you're paying cash or that you have your own financing arranged as you're working the deal on the <u>front end</u>. When asked about cash or financing just say "we'll deal with that later - I'm just looking for your best price".

Now let's talk about how the <u>Business Manager</u> is paid. In most cases, they just get a small salary, with the bulk of their pay coming from a percentage of the Department Profits

A good Business Manager can average anywhere from $500 to $4,500 of <u>profit</u> per vehicle, depending on the type of vehicle and how skilled the customer is in dealing with him. They are paid very well by the dealer to make sure that profit is made in their department. After reading this, you will be skilled also in your dealings with your Business Manager.

As we are nearing the end of this chapter I have five or six things I want to give you a heads up on.

1. When the dealer says "No Payments For 90 Days" - that's true, but built into your loan is the interest or finance charge for those 90 days.

2. "0%" APR (annual percentage rate) or Rebate - which is best? You will have to do the math on this. Sometime the term is short and your payments high. How large is the rebate? What would the finance charge be at the normal rate? Compare to "0%" APR and the rebate savings. In most cases you must choose either the rebate or "0%" APR.

3. A few Business Managers are not totally honest and may try to Pack Your Payment. This means they may include something and not ask you to buy it, but just include it in your monthly payment. As you're signing papers, they will disclose to you quietly that your payment includes this item without selling it to you. Because of tactics like these, you must read everything very carefully; checking that the numbers are what they should be on all documents and only items you purchased are included. Ask questions about anything that doesn't seem right.

4. Spot Delivery is when the dealer wants to deliver the vehicle right now;

as soon as possible after you have said "okay, I'll take it". If the dealer is doing the financing of your vehicle, don't do a spot delivery unless your loan is <u>approved</u> and you know exactly what your interest rate.

5. If your trade-in has a payoff to your old bank, make sure it's shown on all paperwork.

6. If you think you may have bad credit, go to your own credit union or bank first to see how bad it is, and if you can even buy a vehicle.

In ending, just remember, while in the <u>Business Office</u> - before you decide if any of their products work for you, you need to know what they are, and what they do for you. There are quite a few products that the dealer sells and they all contain <u>profit</u>.

Your job as a consumer is to keep that profit down as low as possible and allow the dealer only a <u>fair</u> profit on the products that you do decide to purchase. As you negotiate buying any of these Business Office products, always start low (make them an offer) and go up slowly, they are starting high and will come down.

IMPORTANT ITEMS TO REMEMBER

- ❖ Know And Understand the Difference Between Front End Profit And Back End Profit.

- ❖ Don't Purchase anything but Factory Extended Warranty (if you want an extended warranty).

- ❖ Make Sure The Amount Financed Is The Correct Amount.

- ❖ If you think you have bad credit, check it first at your credit union or bank.

YOUR NOTES

CHAPTER EIGHT

Here We Go To The Dealership

My goal in this chapter is to cover a few last minute things before you venture out on your trip to the dealership to buy your vehicle:

❖ Best Time To Buy
❖ Popular Models & Makes Will Always Cost More
❖ Don't Buy "As Is" (used) Vehicles
❖ Negotiating
❖ Relationship With Your Salesman
❖ Commissions
❖ Dishonesty and Honesty
❖ State Attorney Generals' Office
❖ What To Take With You
❖ How To Do Your Deal
❖ Your Savings

Are you ready? Here we go!

Best Time To Buy
The best times to buy vehicles are week days, preferably in the morning

The best time of the month is at the end, such as the last three days or so.

The best month to buy is right after Christmas and before New Years Day.

The dealer is much more motivated to work with you during the above times, but anytime you go, using my method, you'll do very well for yourself.

The vehicles that you can get the best deal on are what are called in the industry 'bread and butter' vehicles (common, everyday good sellers). Popular vehicles that are in short supply will be much harder to get a <u>great</u> deal on.

<u>NEVER</u> buy an "as is" vehicle from a dealership. Always get some kind of warranty, even if it's just thirty (30) days. The only time you should buy 'as is' is when buying from a private owner, when you don't have any choice in the matter.

Used Vehicles that have been on the car lot for sixty (60) to ninety (90) days will be easier to get a deal on. To find out how long they have had it, without asking the salesman, ask to see the service and repair bills from when it came in. By looking at the date on the bills, you will know how long they've had it.

Treat negotiating as a <u>GAME</u>. Learn to play their game. Don't be a hot-head or give in under pressure. They want to sell a vehicle and make as much money as they can, but they will sell for less, to move the vehicle off the lot. Your part in the game is to negotiate, starting low and going up slowly. If you follow my advice, you'll see that negotiating is an art and can be fun.

Don't get too friendly or personal with your salesperson. Everything you say or talk about goes right back to his manager working your deal to possibly be used against you. And whatever you do, don't act excited or 'in love' with the vehicle.

Commissions for the sales people vary from dealer to dealer. They usually range from 20% to 40% of the profit made on your sale.

Most dealers, business managers and salespeople are honest, but unfortunately, there are always going to be a few 'bad apples' out there who are not. To help you pick an honest dealership, check on-line for comments about them. Also check the State Attorney Generals' Office for complaints against them.

If you have a serious problem with any dealer after you have bought a vehicle from them, tell them you're going to notify the State Attorney Generals' Office - they will work diligently with you to solve your problem as quickly as possible!

In my opinion, the best dealership I worked at in my thirty-five (35) years was "Village

Motors" in Millersburg, Ohio. The owners, Tom Green and Marc Miller, were honest and trustworthy. I enjoyed my job as business manager the ten (10) years I worked for them.

The three main methods to buying a vehicle, new or used, are on the dealership internet, on the phone and in person.

First, let's start with using the dealership internet. You must know which vehicle you want when picking new vehicles. Choose three or four dealerships in your area. Contact the internet manager <u>through the internet.</u>

Tell them you know what the invoice price is, minus all rebates and incentives. Ask him how much better he can do than that! Be sure and keep copies <u>all</u> copies of the emails they send you. You will need them later when you go into the dealership.

Once you get your best price from one of the dealers, contact the other dealers and ask them if they can beat that price. Keep doing this until you have the very best price.

Remember to always ask for the "**Out the Door**" price. This includes all taxes, plate transfer, fees, etc… Some dealers may cut the price on their fees to give you a better "Out the Door" price.

As you're doing this, don't hesitate to tell each dealer that you're working with other dealers. Getting the dealers to compete against each other will get you the very best price. Now make an appointment to go in and buy from the dealer with the best price.

DO NOT tell them if you have a trade-in until you arrive at the dealership. This works the best in getting discount numbers on your deal. If you are trading in a vehicle, the dealer with the best trade in price and the best discount price "out the door" will win your business.

Now for a used vehicle - do the same thing! Choose three or four vehicles you like at three or four different dealers on the internet. Negotiate the same way, using your used vehicle wholesale values. Remember, you want to get the dealers to compete for your business.

If you choose to buy on the phone, BEWARE. They will probably tell you to just come in because they will beat any other deal! You don't want this because you must get the dealers to compete against each other -on the phone, as on the internet - to get your very best possible deal.

Now the last way to buy would be in person. The disadvantage to buying in person is you must physically go to three or four dealers, getting their best deal and then going back to the others to see if they can beat it. This may require several visits to each dealer which is time consuming. It can all be done much easier through the internet or on the phone.

Remember, as you are negotiating, **YOU ARE IN CONTROL**, on the phone, through the internet or at the dealership. You have the ability to walk out, hang up the phone or not answer them on the internet. They won't like this - they are used to being in total control.

When you're ready and heading for your dealership to buy your vehicle, take the following items with you:

1. Drivers License
2. Proof of Insurance
3. State Registration For Your Vehicle/License Plates
4. Title For Your Trade-In Vehicle
5. Any Money You May Be Putting Down On Your Purchase

All states are different - ask your dealer, before going in, what else you will need.

Try to always be fair but firm with the dealers. This will tell them that you know what you're doing. Remember, they must sell vehicles, large or small profit, the numbers work out for them, but they <u>must</u> sell vehicles.

~~~~~~

In the forward of this book I related a true story to you about a customer at a dealership who bought a truck and the dealer made $10,000 profit on the sale.

Now I'm going to break it down for you so you can see exactly how it was done!

Original Profit

Profit on Truck	$3,800.00
Profit on Trade-In	$2,000.00
Profit on Dealer Financing	$1,800.00
($45,000 to finance @ 4% reserve to dealer)	
Profit on Extended Warranty	$900.00
Profit on Credit Life - Disability Insurance	$600.00
Profit on Paint Sealant	$350.00
Profit on GAP Coverage	$300.00
Profit on Glass Etching - Theft Protection	$275.00
TOTAL PROFIT	**$10,025.00**

Now let me show you how much he could have saved by using the information in this book.

Using This Information

Profit on Truck	$500.00
Profit on Trade-In	$0.00
Profit on Dealer Financing (providing your own financing)	$0.00
Profit on Extended Warranty	$200.00 (in most states)
Profit on Credit Life - Disability Insurance (Sale Price & Profit controlled by State Insurance Commission)	$600.00
Profit on Paint Sealant	$100.00
Profit on GAP Coverage	$100.00
Profit on Glass Etching - Theft Protection	$100.00
TOTAL PROFIT	**$1,600.00**

This could have given him a savings amount of **$8,425.00**. WOW !

If there is anything you don't understand, something that comes up when you're trying to make your deal at the dealership or buying from a private party, you can contact me via email at:

larrylewis933@gmail.com

I have read many books on this subject. Some are very good, some are not. But they all had one thing in common - they were too long and went into the day-to-day details of the vehicle sales business. You will never need this much information. You only need to know how to save money!

I have tried to keep it informative and to the point. Are you ready to go out and get that deal? Okay, let's go!

IMPORTANT ITEMS TO REMEMBER

❖ The best time to purchase a vehicle is mornings, week days, end of the month and between Christmas and New Years Day.

❖ Your best deal will be on common, everyday vehicles.

❖ Never buy a vehicle "as is".

❖ Vehicles on the lot sixty to ninety days can be purchased cheaper.

❖ Fully understand how the negotiation process works.

❖ Don't get too friendly with the salesperson.

❖ The State Attorney General can help you with problems.

❖ Your best deal will be through the Dealership Internet Department.

❖ The fees the dealer charges you at the time of delivery are almost ALL profit!

❖ Don't tell them you're trading in a vehicle - wait until you have your best deal made, then tell them.

❖ Never put money down on a vehicle to hold it. Only give them money when your deal is done and you are taking delivery.

❖ I would say good luck here, at the end of this book, but you don't need luck. You now have the knowledge necessary to win the game of negotiation and save thousands on your next vehicle purchase!

And, of course, last but certainly not least:

❖ YOU ARE IN CONTROL!

YOUR NOTES

GLOSSARY

Accident, Health and Disability Insurance : Pays off your loan if you're sick, hurt or disabled

Acquisition Fee : dealer fee to do a lease

Add-On Window Sticker : dealer adds optional equipment directly to the window sticker price

APR : Annual Percentage Rate

As-Is : customer agrees to accept the vehicle in its' current condition without any warranties or guaranties

Back End Profit : profit made when a business manager sells you items when the paperwork on your purchase is being written up

Buying Figure : invoice price minus rebates and incentives

Capitalized Cost Reduction : rebates, trade-in and cash paid down

Car Fax : gives the history of the car such as accidents or repairs

Closed End Lease : the actual value of the vehicle at the end of the lease that is at the risk of the lease company - not the customer

Commission : money made on a sale, usually by the salesperson

Contract : paperwork that spells out all the details of the purchase of the vehicle

Credit Life Insurance :   If you die or are killed, pays off your loan

Dealership : business that sells vehicles

Depreciation : downgrade in the value of a vehicle

Down Payment : cash paid on a vehicle purchase

Early Termination Fee : dealer fee to terminate a lease early

Extended Warranty : coverage extends the time limit and miles for warranty coverage on your vehicle

Finance Charge : percentage of the total amount you are borrowing from a lending institution for your loan

Front End Profit : profit made when a dealer sells you any vehicle

GAP Coverage : pays the difference between what the insurance company pays you and what you owe the financing institution should you total the vehicle

Gross Capitalized Cost : purchase price of the vehicle

Holdback : 2% to 3% of the vehicle MSRP or invoice, paid to the dealer by the factory quarterly each year

Lease End Value : value of vehicle at the end of the lease

Leasee : person leasing the vehicle

Leasor : bank, factory or company that owns the vehicle to be leased

Money Factor : interest or finance charge on a lease

MSRP : window sticker price or retail price

Negotiation : to compromise or find a middle ground agreeable to both parties

Net Capitalized Cost : new total price after all rebates, trade-in and cash paid down

Open End Lease : the value of the vehicle at the end of the lease is the responsibility of the customer

Out The Door Price : price that includes all taxes, plate transfer, fees, etc...

Pay-Off : amount still due on trade-in vehicle

Pre-Paid Lease : all monies due on the lease are paid up front

Rebate : incentive

Residual Value : The percentage of the MSRP (window sticker) that the Leasing Company figures to be the value of the vehicle at the end of the lease

Residualized Accessories : Items added to your vehicle that raises the value and the residual value such as sunroof, spoiler, stereo upgrades, etc.

Retail Price : MSRP / window sticker price

Retail Value : what a dealer could expect to sell your trade-in vehicle for

Salvage Title : title to a vehicle that has been totaled by the insurance company

Security Deposit : deposit usually equal to a monthly payment in a lease agreement

Spot Delivery : when the dealer wants to deliver the vehicle 'on the spot'

Theft Protection : security alarm or glass etching

Trade-In Value : what a dealer will give you for your vehicle on a trade for another vehicle minus clean up costs, mechanic repairs, tire replacement, paint work, etc.

Warranty : protection for the cost of vehicle failures for the customer

Window Sticker Price : the price of the vehicle posted on the window

www.ingramcontent.com/pod-product-compliance
Lightning Source LLC
Chambersburg PA
CBHW071818020426
42331CB00007B/1532